COMPOSER SHOWCASE
HAL LEONARD
STUDENT PIANO LIBRARY

EARL

Think Jazz!
A JAZZ PIANO METHOD

BY BILL BOYD

Editor: Barbara Kreader

ISBN 978-0-7935-2318-4

HAL•LEONARD®
CORPORATION
7777 W. BLUEMOUND RD. P.O. BOX 13819 MILWAUKEE, WI 53213

Copyright © 1994 by HAL LEONARD CORPORATION
International Copyright Secured All Rights Reserved

For all works contained herein:
Unauthorized copying, arranging, adapting, recording or public performance is an infringement of copyright.
Infringers are liable under the law.

Visit Hal Leonard Online at
www.halleonard.com

TO THE STUDENT

Welcome to the world of jazz piano. In this book, you will learn about many different jazz styles from the ragtime music of the 1900s to the rock styles of today. In addition, you will encounter many improvisation experiences, including the blues. By the time you complete this book you will have enough chord knowledge to improvise accompaniments for popular songs. Good luck and enjoy.

TO THE TEACHER

This book will complement and provide supplementary material for any standard piano method. No background in jazz or improvisation is required to teach this method successfully.

The student is introduced to several jazz styles and improvisation through exercises and compositions that emphasize interpretation. Although the material is presented sequentially, it is not organized into units or chapters. This will enable you to have discussions and make assignments according to the readiness of the student and to your priorities and goals. As with any method, the music is within one grade level but does progress in difficulty.

The various compositions in this book sound in style because of the jazz rhythms. Rote teaching of these rhythms is permissible at this level. An interesting and detailed approach to understanding jazz rhythms is included for study when the student is ready.

Think Jazz!

CONTENTS

Rock Eighth Notes

Eighth notes in rock music are played evenly as they are in classical music. Often at the beginning of a rock song you will see:

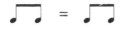

Moderate To Fast Rock Songs

Quarter notes are played staccato . . . . but not as staccato as in classical music. Jazz musicians sometimes use the word "spaced" to describe this quarter-note style.

Space the quarter notes in the following piece.

THE ROCK EXCHANGE

INTERPRETATION (the musical style in which a piece is performed): In rock style pieces place slight accents on the second and fourth beats. Observe accents and slurs, noticing that measures with four quarter notes need no accents.

UNDER THE ROCK

Swing Eighth Notes

Eighth notes in swing style jazz are WRITTEN evenly as in classical music but are PLAYED unevenly.

The example below is the first two measures of "I've Been Workin' On The Railroad." Play the eighth notes the way you would sing this song and you will be playing uneven swing eighth notes.

Play "Row, Row, Row Your Boat" as you would sing it!

Notice that the first note of each eighth-note group is played longer than the second note.

Here is another way to think about uneven swing eighth notes.

Eighth-note triplets are played three even notes to the beat. Say the word "strawberry" as you play triplets with your right hand and quarter notes with your left hand.

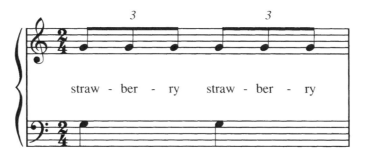

Or count . . . . . .

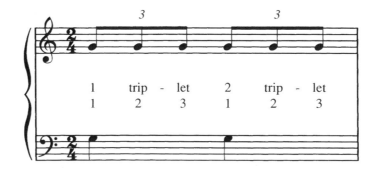

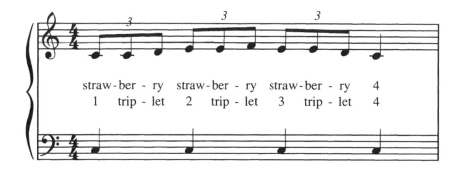

Tie the first two notes of the triplet together. The resulting rhythm is the swing eighth note feeling.

The triplet rhythm with the first two notes tied together may be written:

Once the swing eighth note feeling is achieved, the counting may revert back to "one and two and . . ."

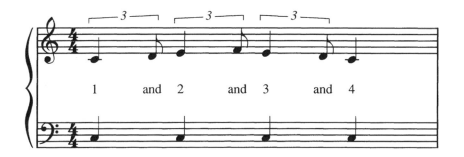

SUMMARY:

Play the following with swing eighth notes. Swing eighths are usually played legato.

EIGHTH-NOTE SWING

Jazz Rhythms

Melodies may be "jazzed up" by changing the original rhythm. Consider the simple melody from "Mary Had A Little Lamb."

In the example below the half notes are played half a beat SOONER on the "and" of beat two. This jazz rhythm is called the ANTICIPATED beat.

In the following example the first note of the song is played half a beat LATER on the "and" of beat one. This jazz rhythm is called the DELAYED beat.

Another word for these jazz rhythms is SYNCOPATION.

Below are the first two measures of the next song, "Over Easy." In the first example the quarter notes are played ON beats two and three.

In the following example the second quarter note is played half a beat BEFORE beat three as it appears in the song.

Notes played on an "and" (upbeat) and tied into a downbeat are slightly accented.

INTERPRETATION: Place slight accents on the anticipated beats.

OVER EASY

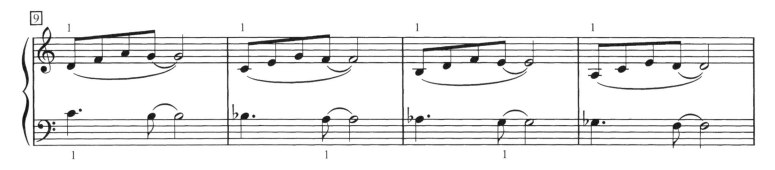

Copyright © 1990 by HAL LEONARD CORPORATION
International Copyright Secured   All Rights Reserved

INTERPRETATION: The anticipated beat rhythm of "Rock-A-Bye" is the same as the rhythm of "Over Easy"•The eighth notes are played EVENLY and more legato in slow rock songs•The accent rule for the anticipated beat should be observed•The quarter notes on the fourth beat in the left hand receive slight accents.

ROCK-A-BYE

Copyright © 1990 by HAL LEONARD CORPORATION
International Copyright Secured   All Rights Reserved

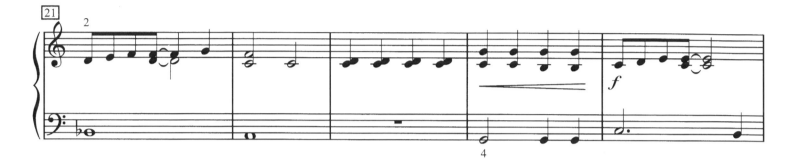

Rock songs often use the dotted quarter and eighth rhythm in the left-hand bass part.

1 + 2 +   3 + 4 +

SLOW ROCK

gradually get softer

p

In faster rock music the dotted quarter and eighth notes are spaced.

Written: Played:

$1 + 2 + 3 + 4 + \quad 1 + 2 + 3 + 4 +$

INTERPRETATION: Space all quarter notes.

BASS(IC) ROCK

Moderately Fast Rock

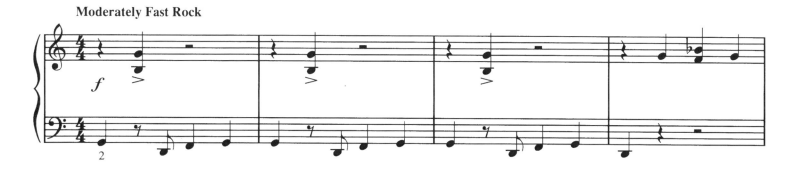

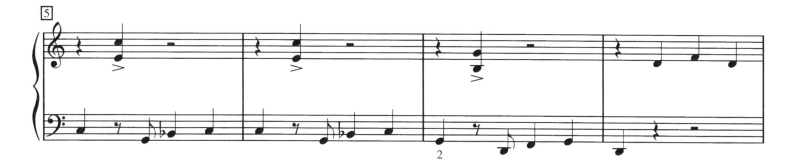

So often in jazz music the interpretation (the style or way you play) is not indicated in the music.
The jazz musician needs to know how to properly interpret the music.

Things To Remember

Rock Style

Play even eighth notes.
Space quarter notes in moderate to fast songs.
Play eighth notes legato in slow tempo.
Quarter notes may or may not be spaced in a slow tempo.
Slight accents are sometimes placed on beats two and four.

The often-used bass rhythm ♩. ♪♩ is played as written in a slow tempo.

In a fast tempo it is played as ♩ 𝄾 ♪♩

Swing Style

Eighth note interpretation: written: ♪♪ played: ♪³♪

Eighth notes are usually played legato.
Slight accents are sometimes placed on beats two and four in moderate to fast songs.
Quarter notes are often spaced in moderate to fast songs.

Rhythm

Anticipated beat: ♩ ♪♩♩

Notes that fall on an upbeat and are tied into a downbeat receive slight accents (anticipated beats).

Delayed beat: 𝄾 ♪♩ ♩

Delayed beats are often accented.

Chords

The jazz musician uses chords for improvisation. Chords are constructed from scales.

Major Chords

FORMULA: Major chords combine the first, third, and fifth notes from the major scale. When the major scale is used for chord construction it is called the CHORD SCALE.

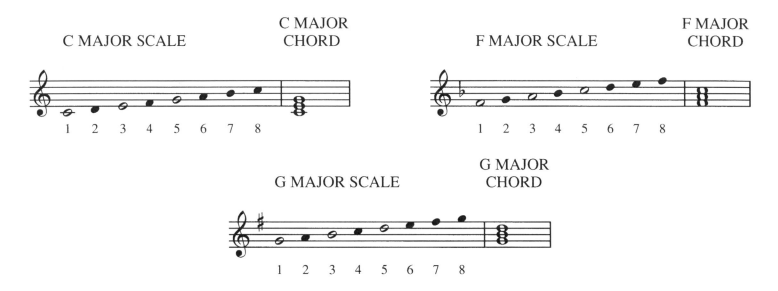

Chords containing three notes are called TRIADS. The first note of the chord is called the ROOT. The remaining notes are identified in terms of their relationship to the root.

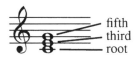

A letter placed over a measure indicates the chord to be played for that measure. When no letter appears, the chord from the measure before is played. This letter is called a CHORD SYMBOL and stands for a major triad.

A chord is in ROOT POSITION when the root appears as the bottom note. The chord may be INVERTED by placing other chord tones on the bottom.

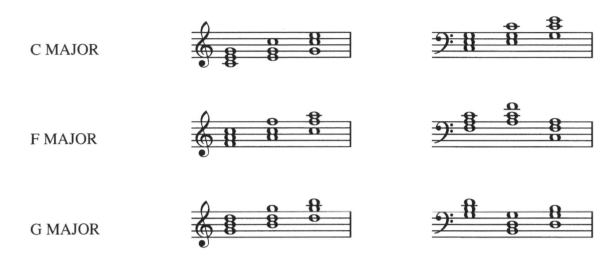

C MAJOR

F MAJOR

G MAJOR

Improvising With Chords

Left-Hand Improvisation

The jazz musician learns to improvise accompaniments based on the chord symbols. The chords for many songs move from C to F to G.

At first it is wise to avoid big left-hand skips. Select chord positions or inversions that are close to one another.

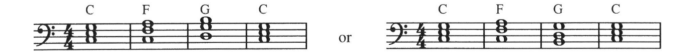

or

In the following examples notice how the chords form various types of accompaniments.

Three-Four Time

ON TOP OF OLD SMOKY

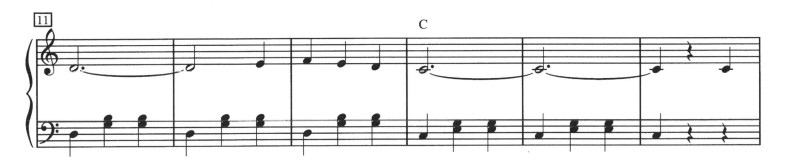

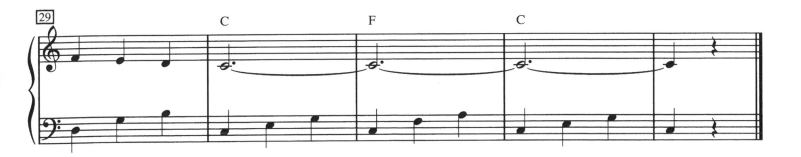

Four-Four Time

Below are several accompaniment patterns based upon the C chord.

TRADITIONAL:

THIS OLD MAN

ROCK:

Slow Rock

Fast Rock

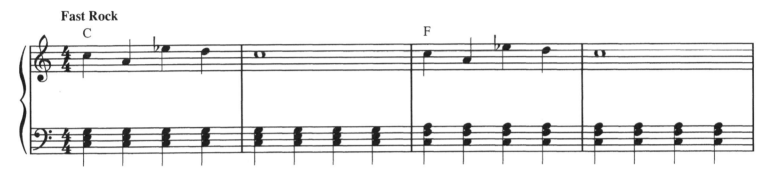

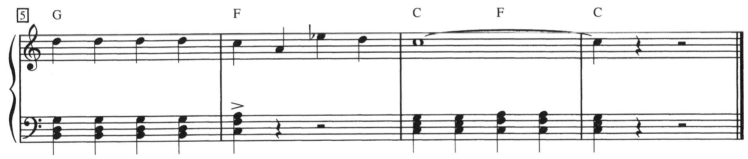

Additional rock accompaniments may be developed by playing the chord root in the left hand and the chord in the right hand.

The following song is based on chord tones. The rhythm in the left hand on line two is easy if you match it up with the right-hand notes.

TRIADS FROM TRINIDAD

Right-Hand Chord Tone Improvisation

Memorize the C, F and G chords and inversions:

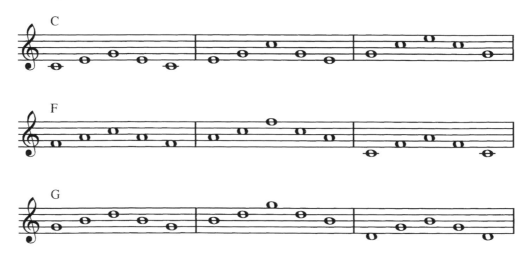

Study and play the sample improvisations.

Now it's your turn! Improvise, ending your improvisation on "C."

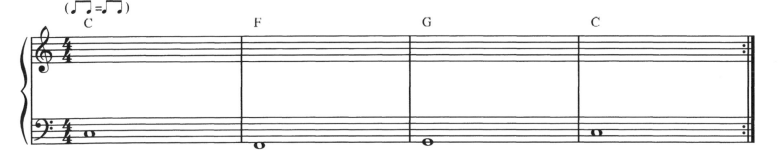

As you go through the book, memorize all of the chords in the exercises and songs. The jazz musician continually builds a chord vocabulary.

The Dominant-Seventh Chord

FORMULA: Combine the 1 3 5 ♭7 notes of the major scale.

CHORD SYMBOL: C7

INVERSIONS:

For ease of playing, jazz musicians frequently omit notes in accompaniment patterns, but the third and flat seventh notes should always be present.

More Traditional Accompaniments

Replay "On Top Of Old Smoky" (pg. 18) and "This Old Man" (pg. 20). Whenever the G chord is indicated, play a G7 instead.

Memorize the C, F and G7 chords and improvise an accompaniment for "Skater's Waltz".

SKATER'S WALTZ

Invent some of your own accompaniments for "Skater's Waltz".

Improvise accompaniments for the following folk songs:

Clementine
Santa Lucia
Happy Birthday
Down In The Valley

Tom Dooley
He's Got The Whole World In His Hands
Michael, Row The Boat Ashore
The Yellow Rose Of Texas

Jazz Accompaniments

First play "When The Saints Go Marching In" with a traditional accompaniment.

WHEN THE SAINTS GO MARCHING IN

In jazz, playing the flat seventh adds a bluesy quality to the music. Often just the root and the flat seventh are played in the left hand.

Sometimes the sixth note of the chord scale is combined with the flat seventh to create left-hand accompaniment patterns. The sixth is not considered a part of the chord.

Now play this version of "When The Saints Go Marching In", comparing it to the first. Notice the bluesy effect caused by the flat seventh notes.

WHEN THE SAINTS GO MARCHING IN

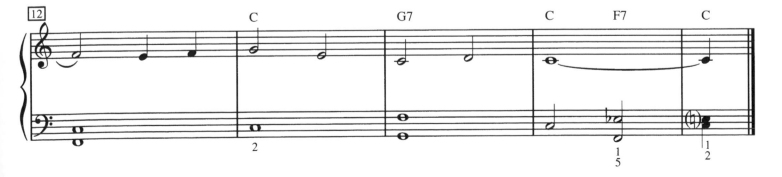

The sixth note of the chord scale may be added to the notes of the dominant-seventh chord to form the following familiar bass pattern.

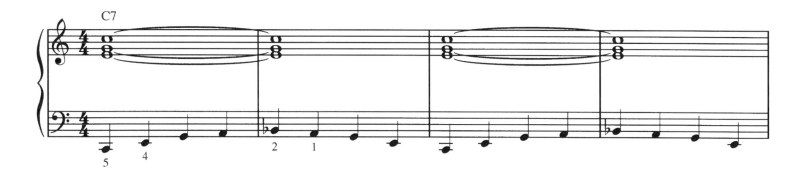

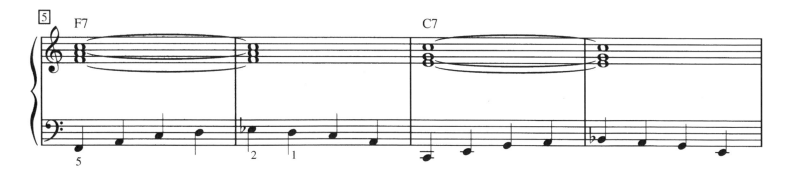

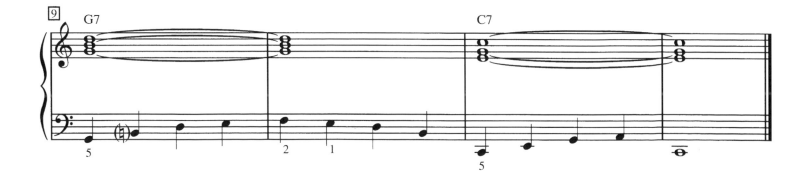

The flat seventh is used to create a typical rock bass pattern.

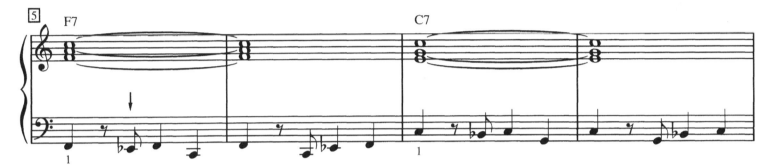

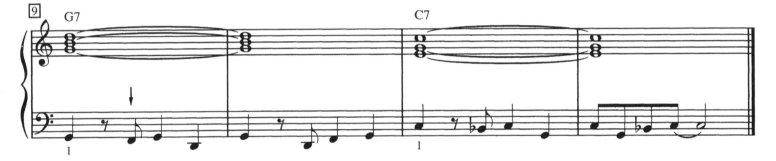

In the following exercise the right hand creates an improvisation using the dominant-seventh chord tones. Notice how the flat seventh note produces a bluesy effect.

In jazz music the dominant-seventh chords in the left-hand accompaniment often appear with just the third and flat seventh.

Jazz pieces are sometimes played in three-four time. The next song, "Blue Waltz", starts with several dominant-seventh chords.

Study the left-hand accompaniment and notice that when the dominant-seventh chords appear, the left hand plays the third and the flat seventh.

INTERPRETATION: Follow the slurring carefully •Observe the dynamics (loud and soft) •Look for the flat seventh notes.

BLUE WALTZ

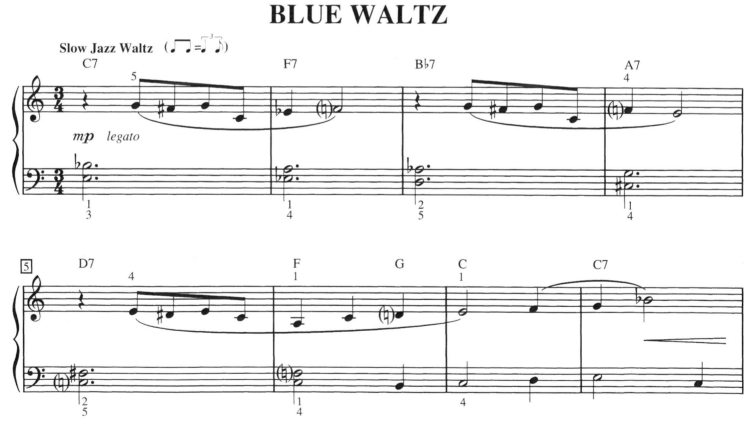

Copyright © 1988 by HAL LEONARD CORPORATION
International Copyright Secured   All Rights Reserved

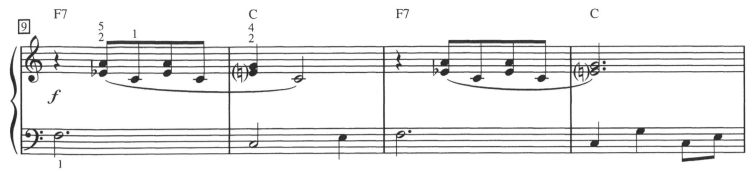

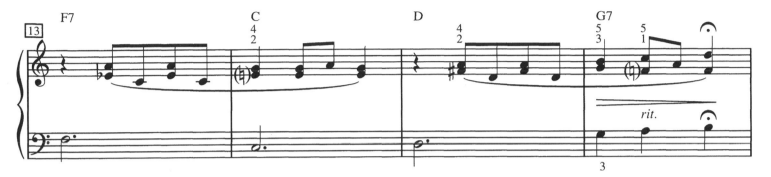

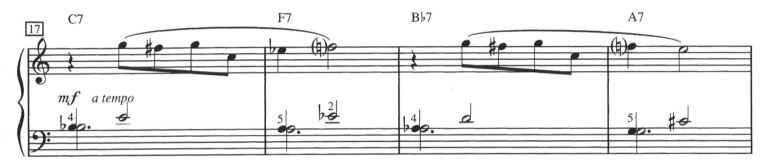

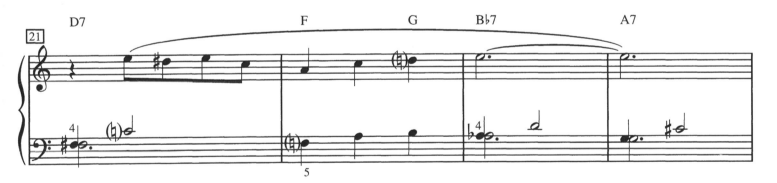

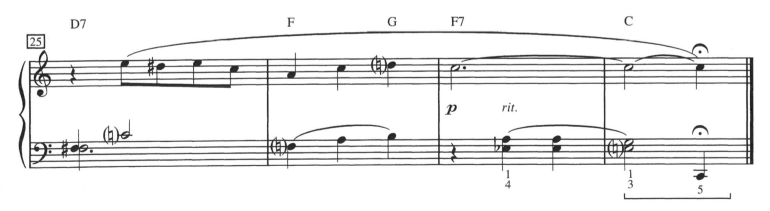

All of the preceding exercises and songs demonstrate familiar jazz sounds. Later you will apply these ideas to your own improvisations.

More Anticipated Beats

When figuring out jazz rhythms, it is sometimes helpful to count out loud and clap or tap the rhythm. In addition, jazz rhythms in the right hand need to be coordinated with the left-hand accompaniments.

Coordination Exercises

Count out loud, keep a steady beat, and go slowly at first. Play even eighth notes. Try each exercise without the tie, then tie the notes as written.

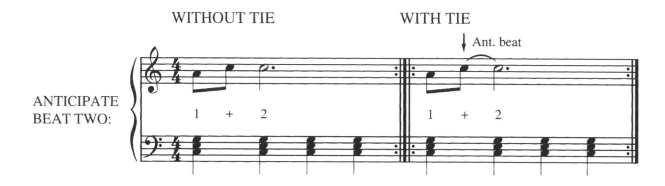

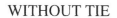

Extend the same rhythm:

ANTICIPATE BEAT ONE:

1 + 2 + 3 + 4 +   1   1 + 2 + 3 + 4 +   1

Eighth-Note Rhythms With The Anticipated Beat

Play each exercise several times with even eighth notes. Then play several times with uneven eighth notes.

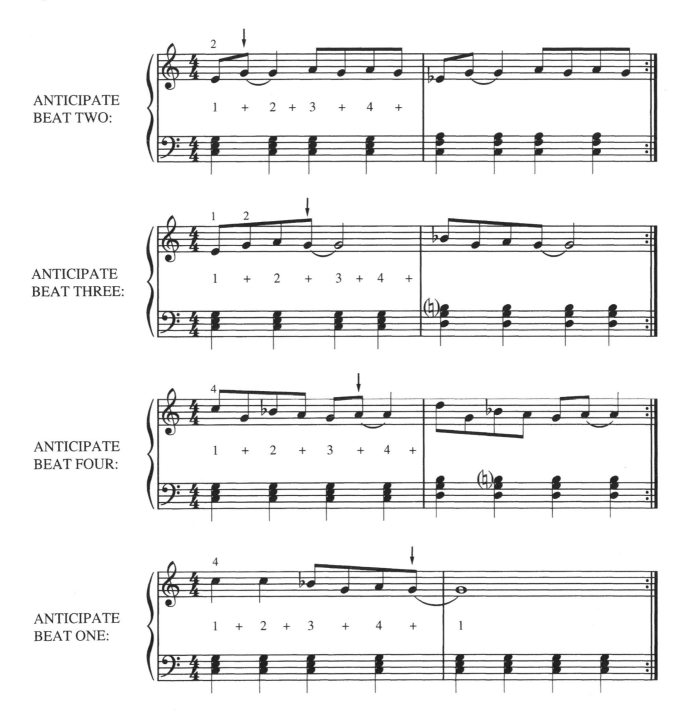

ANTICIPATE BEAT TWO:

1 + 2 + 3 + 4 +

ANTICIPATE BEAT THREE:

1 + 2 + 3 + 4 +

ANTICIPATE BEAT FOUR:

1 + 2 + 3 + 4 +

ANTICIPATE BEAT ONE:

1 + 2 + 3 + 4 +   1

The right-hand part on the next song applies the last rhythm in measures 15 and 16 and looks like this:

Notice that the left-hand part is one of the suggested jazz accompaniments.

INTERPRETATION: Space the quarter notes•Play the eighth notes legato•In measure 11 keep the quarter notes short.

FLAT SEVENTH ROCK

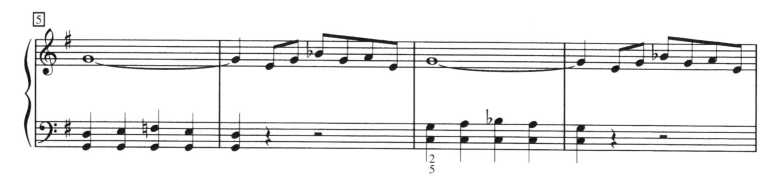

More About Chords And Jazz Rhythms

Chords

Chords are played within the framework of a key. In the example below chords are constructed on each note of the C Major scale.

Roman numerals identify each chord in the scale:

Notice that the C and F chords have the same letter names and notes but the Roman numerals are different in each key.

The C, F and G7 chords are labeled I, IV and V7 in the key of C.

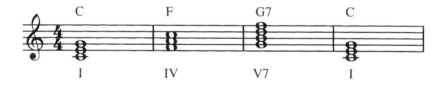

The I, IV and V7 chords are called the PRIMARY chords in any key. Many folk songs, country western, blues, and jazz compositions may be accompanied by these chords.

When one chord moves to another, the movement is called a CHORD PROGRESSION. Jazz musicians talk about chord progressions in terms of letter names and Roman numerals.

Playing Jazz Rhythms

The Anticipated Beat

Two challenges occur when playing anticipated beats:

- •Coordinating the left and right hands.

- •Counting the rhythm when the left hand plays long notes.

In the following exercises, the first two measures challenge coordination, while the second two measures require careful counting.

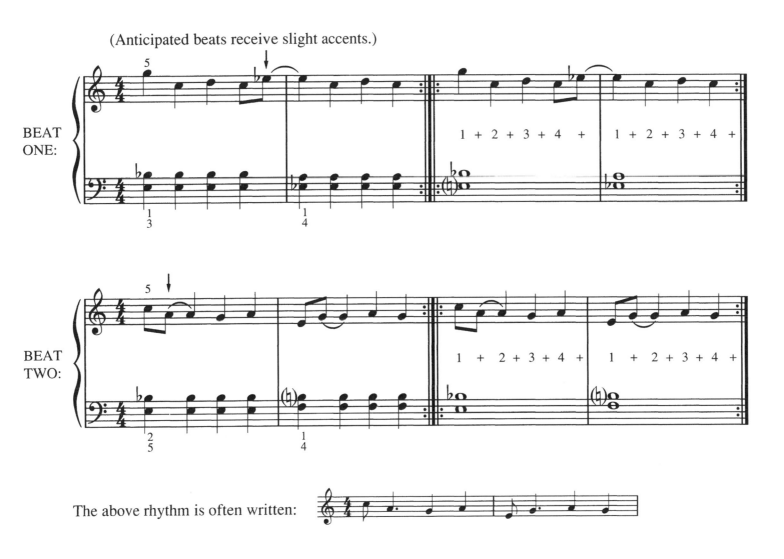

The above rhythm is often written:

BEAT
THREE:

BEAT
FOUR:

The above rhythm is often written:

Eighth Notes

Play both even and uneven eighth notes.

The above rhythm is often written:

The above rhythm is often written:

The following exercises anticipate beats one, two, three and four. Count out loud as you play and space the quarter notes.

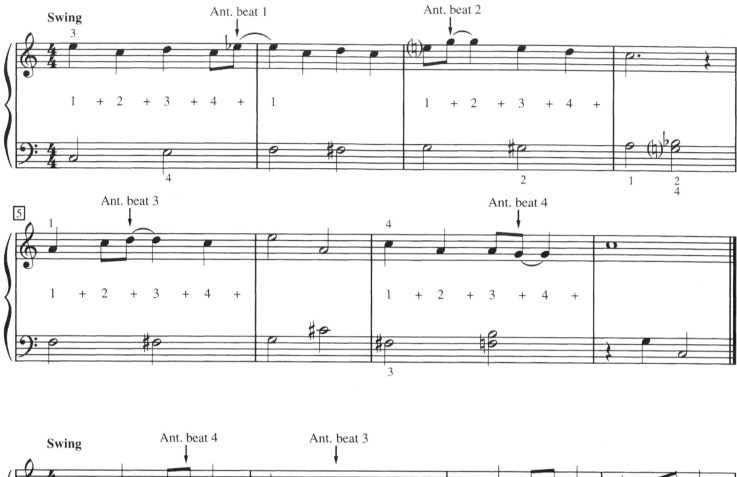

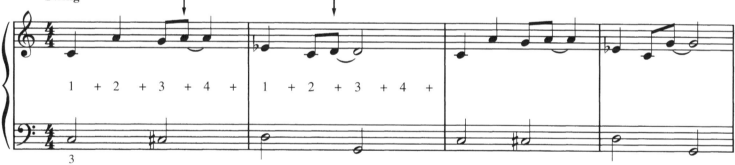

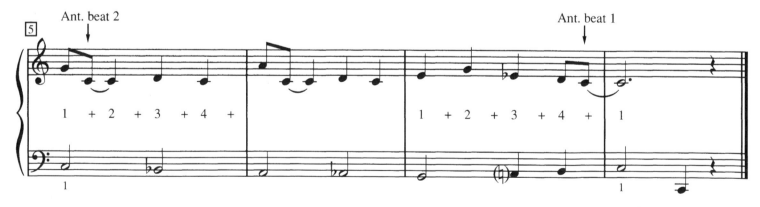

The Blues

The BLUES, a form of jazz that appeared before 1900, is still played today. Many blues styles exist, but what makes the blues sound distinctive?

First—the chord progression. Blues songs and improvisations are twelve measures in length and use the basic chords: I, IV7, and V7 (the primary chords).

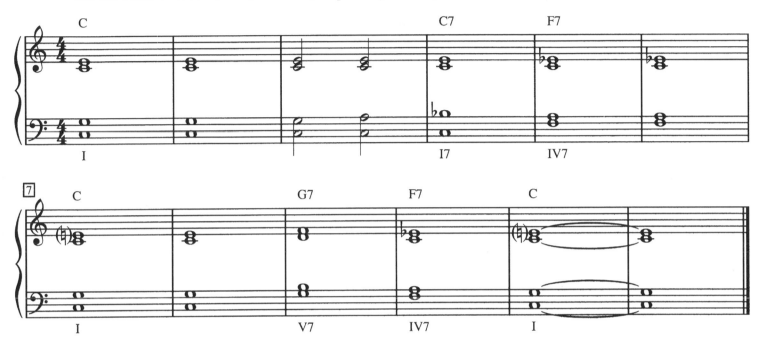

Second—the melody. One might simply say that the melodic sound of the blues is achieved by playing melody notes borrowed from a minor key over the accompaniment chords built from a major key.

C MAJOR SCALE   C MINOR SCALE

A characteristic blues melody would borrow the E♭ and the B♭ from the minor scale.

The E♭ is played by the right hand against an E♮ in the left-hand chord. This combination of major and minor produces the blues sound. We have already discussed how the flat seventh creates a bluesy feeling.

Look at the E♭ and the B♭ in terms of the C major scale. These notes are the flat third and flat seventh. In any key, if the flat third and the flat seventh are played in the right hand, a bluesy feeling will result.

The following exercises emphasize the flat third and the flat seventh in the right-hand blues improvisation. Play uneven swing eighth notes.

BLUES IN C

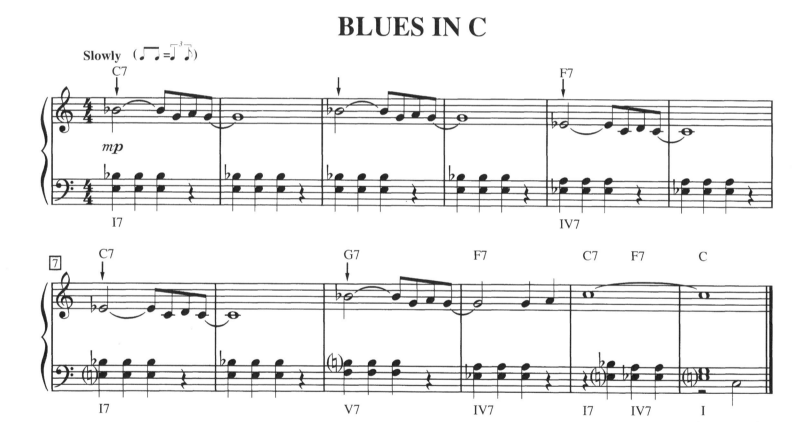

Key of F major:

BLUES IN F

Key of G major:

BLUES IN G

Improvising The Blues

Improvising Left-Hand Accompaniments

Walking Bass

Most bass lines use chord tones and scale tones. The following bass line style is called WALKING BASS and is usually played legato. Possible ways to improvise this left-hand accompaniment include:

1. Using notes of the dominant-seventh chord plus the sixth note of the chord scale.

2. Adding the flat third note to the triad.

3. Adding the sixth note of the chord scale to the triad.

4. Creating a bass line that remains close to one hand position and does not require large skips.

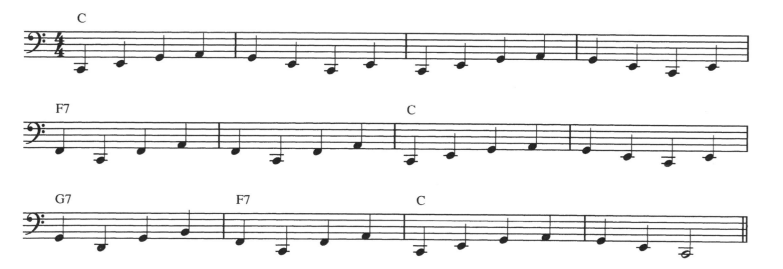

Chordal Accompaniments

5. Triads

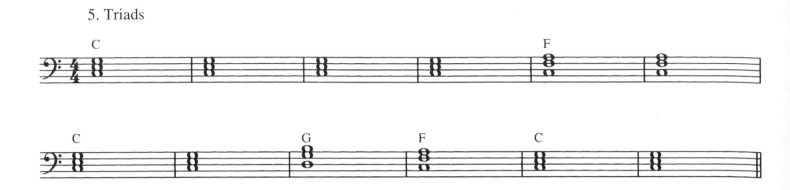

6. Dominant-seventh chord: root and flat seventh.

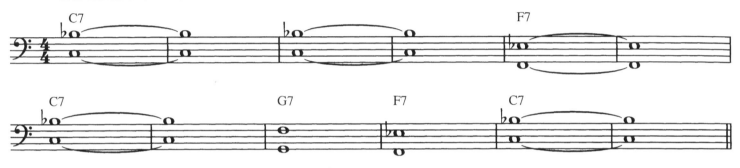

7. Dominant-seventh chord: root and flat seventh with the sixth note of the chord scale.

8. Dominant-seventh chord: third and flat seventh.

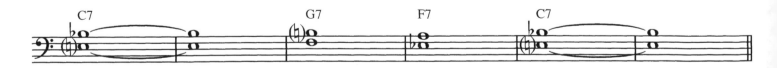

Any of these eight left-hand accompaniments may be played with a right-hand blues improvisation.

Melodic Improvisation

Blues melodic improvisation is based on the notes contained in BLUES SCALES. The following notes are part of the C BLUES SCALE. The first note of any scale is called the TONIC.

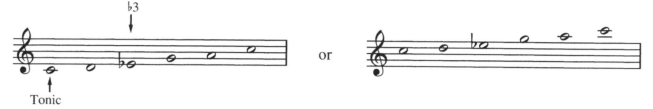

or

Notice that the flat third is a part of this scale.

To create a twelve-measure improvisation think in terms of linking two-measure phrases together.

STEP ONE: Select a two-measure rhythm pattern.

STEP TWO: Select a group of notes from the C blues scale. Begin with three-note groups. The note group must contain the TONIC.

STEP THREE: Combine the note group with the selected rhythm, ending on the TONIC.

RHYTHM PATTERN   NOTE GROUP   COMBINATION

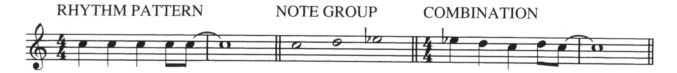

STEP FOUR: Select an accompaniment for the left hand. Repeat the two-measure improvisation six times and play the selected accompaniment.

MORE IDEAS:

RHYTHM PATTERN   NOTE
                   GROUP   COMBINATION

- Start on any note
- End on the tonic
- Play notes in any order
- Play uneven eighth notes
- The direction of the melody must move down after the flat third is played

no   yes

Have a friend or your teacher play the following accompaniment as you play the melodic ideas on page 48. Extend the two-measure ideas to twelve measures by playing the idea six times.

BLUES ACCOMPANIMENT:

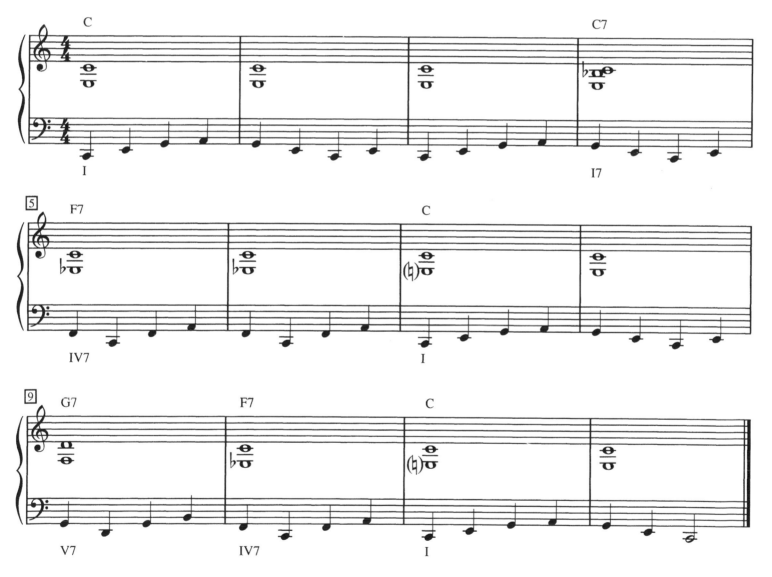

In the next example, melodic idea number five on page 48 is combined with walking bass number three on page 45.

Follow the improvising steps and create your own twelve-measure blues improvisation.

HELPFUL HINTS

- Memorize the blues chord progression and the accompaniment.
- Memorize the C blues scale.
- Begin with small note groups that contain the tonic.
- End the two-measure improvisation on the tonic.

Improvise right hand.

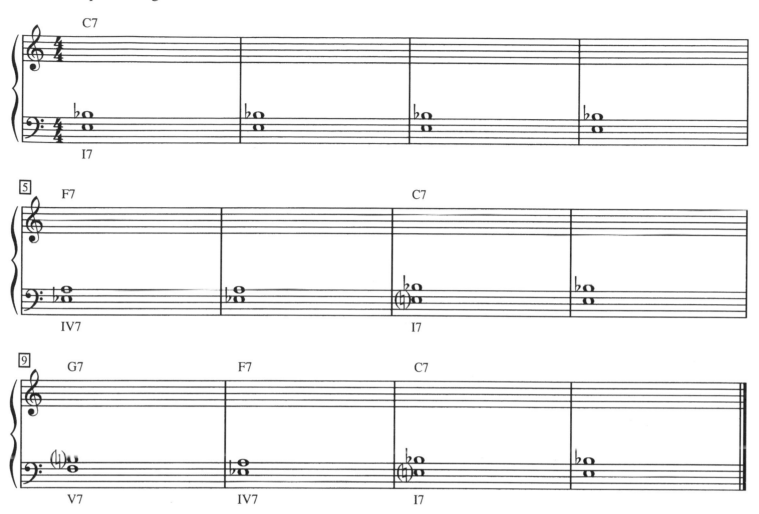

This type of improvisation is called a RIFF. A riff is a short melody repeated over the twelve-measure blues chord progression. Riff playing suggests the swing style of the 40s and rock of the early 50s.

To concentrate on your own melodic ideas without playing the left hand, have a friend or your teacher play the accompaniment once again while you improvise the right hand. Follow the above chart as you improvise.

The right-hand part on the next song is based upon the notes of the C blues scale. The left hand is bass line number two. It has been changed to include the dotted quarter and eighth rhythm for rock style.

BASS LINE   CHANGED FOR ROCK
TWO

52

INTERPRETATION: Space the quarter notes.

BLUES SCALE ROCK

Minor Chords

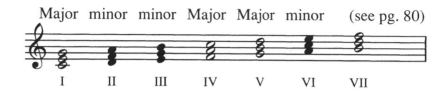

Major minor minor Major Major minor (see pg. 80)

I II III IV V VI VII

Notice that the II, III and VI chords are minor. The small letter "m" equals minor.

FORMULA: Combine the 1, ♭3 and 5 from the major scale. (Use a natural sign to flat a sharped note.)

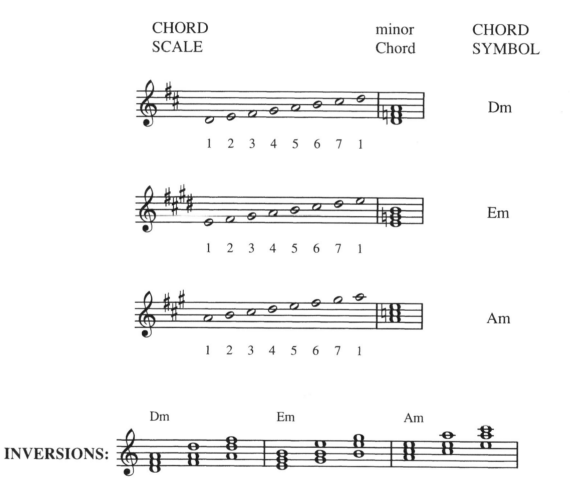

CHORD minor CHORD
SCALE Chord SYMBOL

1 2 3 4 5 6 7 1   Dm

1 2 3 4 5 6 7 1   Em

1 2 3 4 5 6 7 1   Am

INVERSIONS:

Dm   Em   Am

These new chords are combined with the major chords in the following left-hand example. Finger all chords 5 3 1.

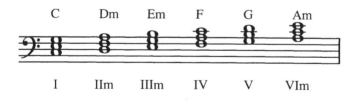

C   Dm   Em   F   G   Am

I   IIm   IIIm   IV   V   VIm

The next song, "Hordes Of Chords," applies all of these chords.

54

INTERPRETATION: Slightly accent anticipated beats•Space quarter notes•Maintain a steady beat•Observe dynamics•Notice that some eighth notes are spaced: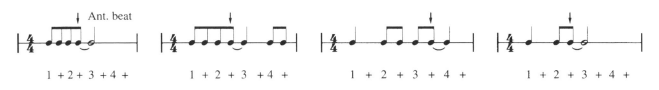

Practice Rhythms:

HORDES OF CHORDS

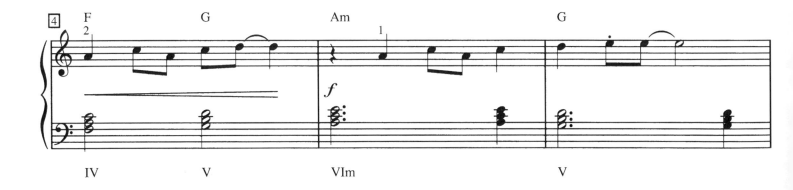

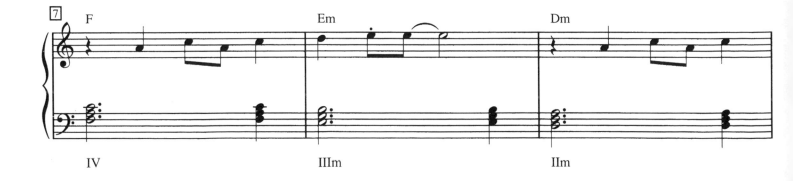

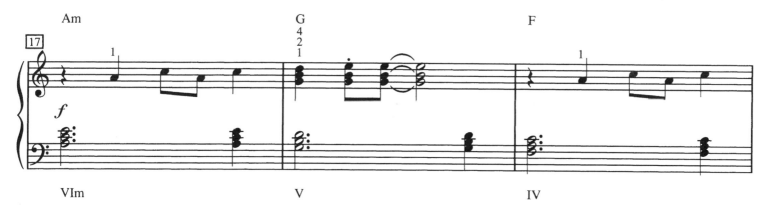

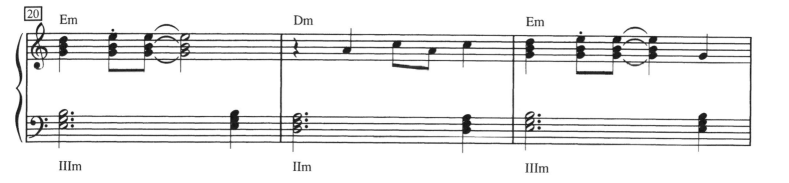

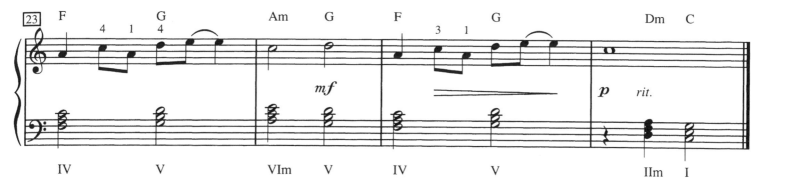

The I-VIm-IIm-V7 chord progression is common to many rock songs of the 50s.

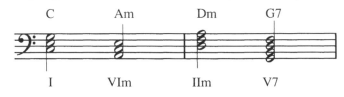

The following example captures the sound of a typical 50s rock ballad. In this period some songs were played with even eighth notes and others with uneven eighths. Try this example both ways.

Improvisation With The Major Scale

The notes of the C major scale will complement this chord progression. Play the sample improvisations with uneven eighth notes.

The second improvisation applies inversions to the Am and G7 chords to avoid wide skips from one chord to the other.

ped. simile

Have a friend or your teacher play the following accompaniment while you improvise with the notes of the C major scale.

Many fast rock songs of the 50s were based on the blues chord progression. The walking bass accompaniment was common.

Slow Rock accompaniment: 50s style

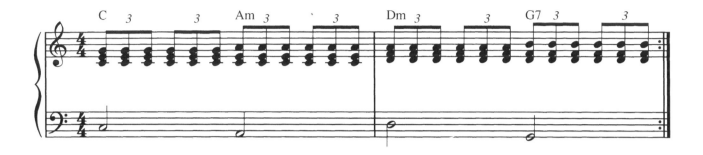

The IV chord may replace the IIm chord.

Fast Rock accompaniment: Space the quarter notes.

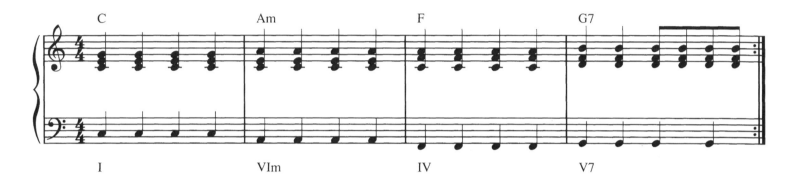

The same accompaniment anticipating beat one:

In a slow rock tempo the dotted quarter and eighth notes are played as written.

Chord Review

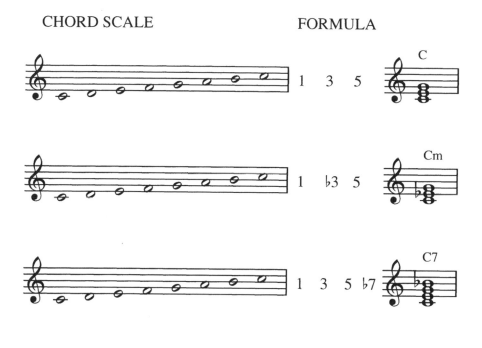

CHORD SCALE   FORMULA

Chord Test

Fill in the chord notes in the blank measures. A complete list of all chords studied in this book appears in the appendix on page 86.

Ragtime

Ragtime is a style of jazz made popular by SCOTT JOPLIN during the early 1900s. This style is usually slow, and the eighth notes are almost always played evenly.

RAGTIME RHYTHM NO. 1

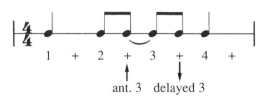

This rhythm contains an anticipated third beat <u>and</u> a delayed third beat. In other words, a note is played BEFORE beat three and AFTER beat three. No note occurs ON beat three.

Let's take this rhythm a step at a time.

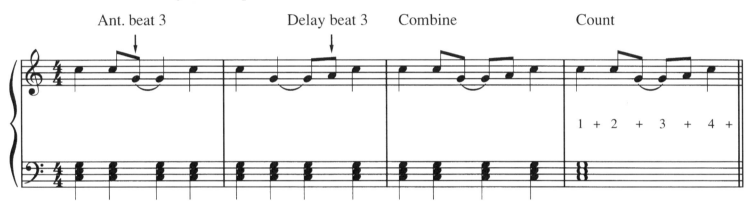

Another way of looking at this rhythm:

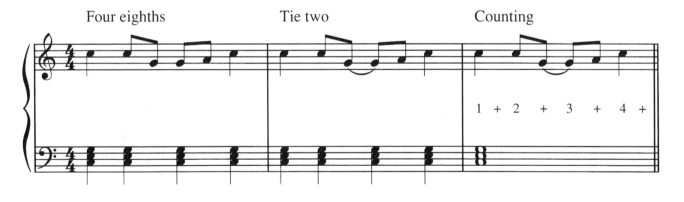

Rhythm number one appears in the opening measures of the next song. The eighth notes are played unevenly, which is an exception to the rule.

INTERPRETATION: Play with a soft gentle style•Maintain a good legato throughout
•Anticipated beats receive a slight accent.

RAGTIME

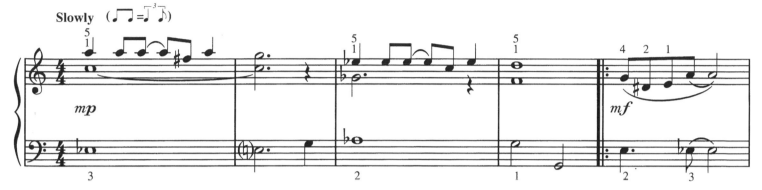

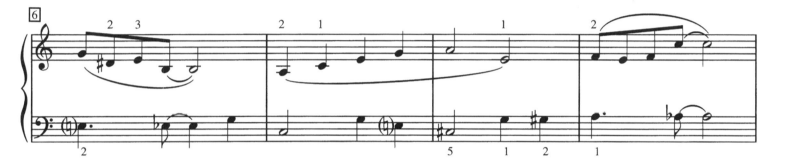

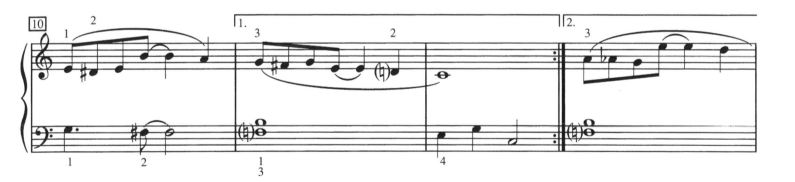

Copyright © 1990 by HAL LEONARD CORPORATION
International Copyright Secured   All Rights Reserved

RAGTIME RHYTHM NO. 2

1 + 2 + 3 + 4 +

This rhythm is the same as rhythm number one except beat two is anticipated and delayed.

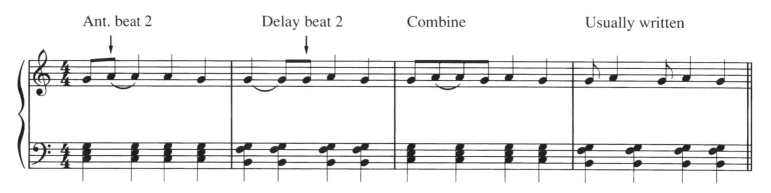

Another way of looking at this rhythm:

Ragtime pieces are often accompanied by a left-hand chord pattern called STRIDE. In stride left-hand style, a single chord tone is played on beats one and three. A chord consisting of two or more tones is played on beats two and four.

Stride left-hand style is played for ragtime, dixieland, and early swing.

Rhythm number one with stride left hand:

The next composition includes rhythms number one and two and demonstrates the stride left hand.

RAG WEED

Measures 19 and 21 look very complicated rhythmically. Actually, this is ragtime rhythm number one (pg. 60) divided between the two hands.

Play the melody of measure number three and divide the notes between the two hands as indicated below.

Now play measure 19 with the same rhythmic feeling.

MEASURE 19

Drill for measure three:

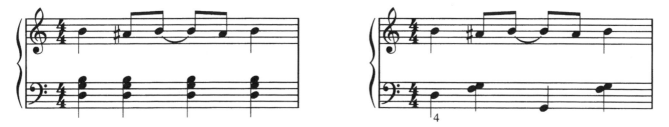

INTERPRETATION: Left-hand stride style always spaced•All eighth and quarter notes spaced unless marked legato•Observe dynamics and maintain a steady beat.

RAG WEED

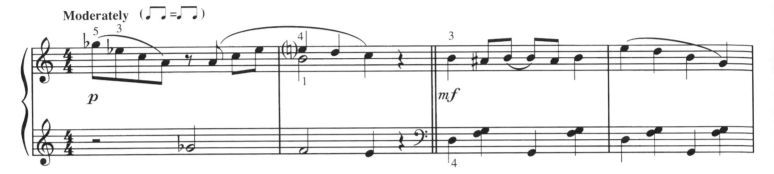

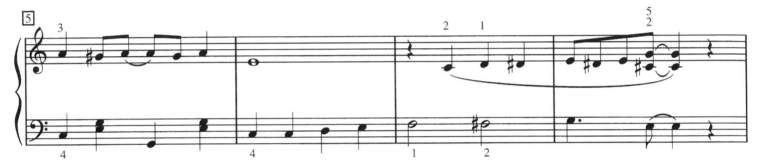

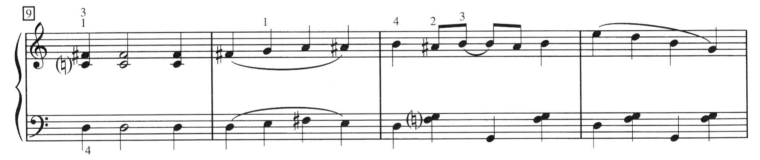

RAGTIME RHYTHM NO. 3

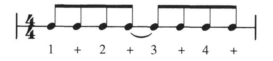

This is the same as ragtime rhythm number one with one exception: eighth notes, instead of quarter notes, are played on beats one and four.

RHYTHM NO. 1   RHYTHM NO. 3

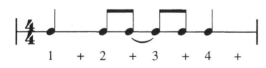

Drill for ragtime rhythm number three:

Counting:

Ragtime rhythm number three with stride left hand:

The next composition includes ragtime rhythms two and three.

INTERPRETATION: Left-hand stride spaced•Quarter and eighth notes spaced•Play left hand louder to emphasize the melody in measures 19–21•Observe dynamics and keep a steady beat.

WET RAG

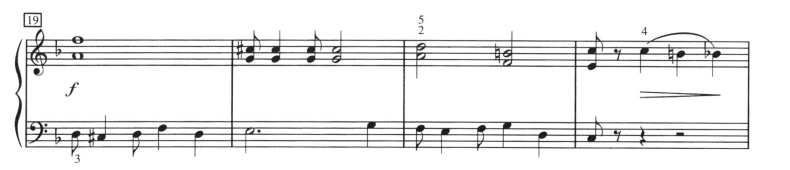

Seventh Chords

Major Seventh Chord

FORMULA: Combine the 1 3 5 7 from the major scale.

CHORD SYMBOL: M7 or Maj7 or Δ

Minor Seventh Chord

FORMULA: Combine the 1 ♭3 5 ♭7 from the major scale.

CHORD SYMBOL: m7 or -7

Fill in the chords in the blank measures below.

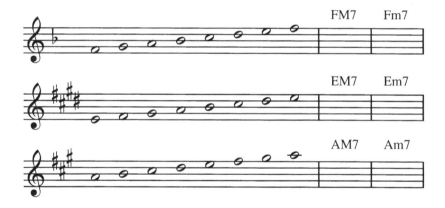

Seventh chords constructed on the notes of the C major scale:

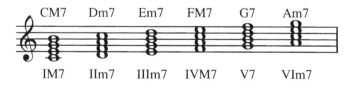

Practice these chords with the left hand. Fingering: 5 3 2 1

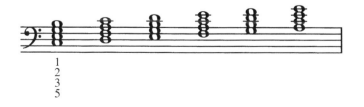

A more modern sound results when seventh chords accompany melodies. The following arrangement of "Marine's Hymn" abandons the traditional harmony and demonstrates the use of seventh chords.

The left-hand accompaniment is in the BLOCK-CHORD STYLE, in which all the notes of the chord are played together.

MARINE'S HYMN

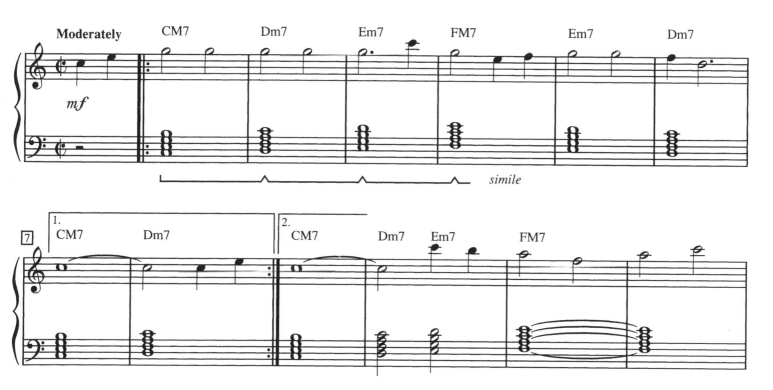

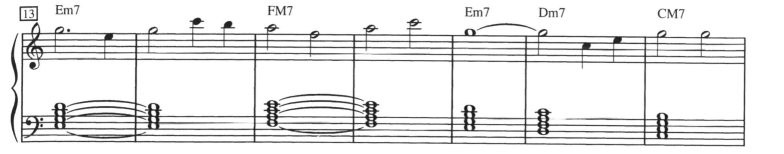

Improvising Left-Hand Accompaniments

"Deck The Hall" with block-chord accompaniment.

DECK THE HALL

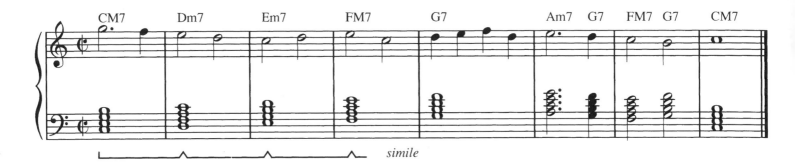

Two more ideas:

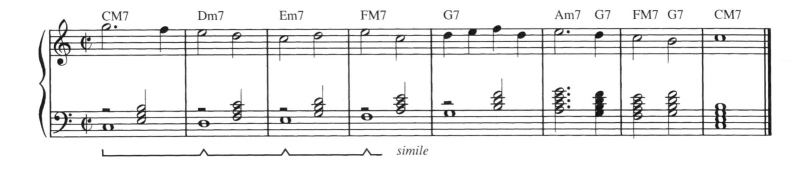

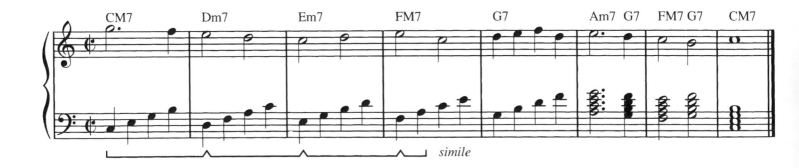

Three-Four Time

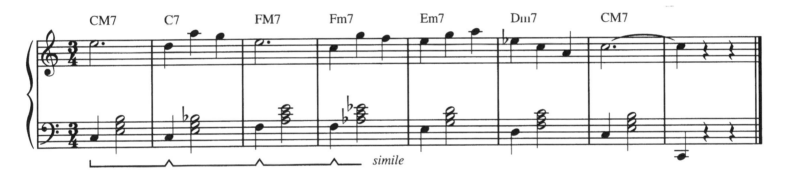

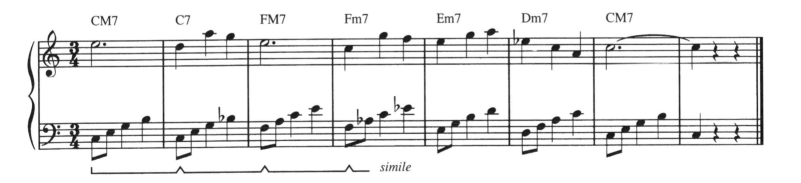

Jazz Grace Notes

Jazz grace notes are usually one half step below the melody note.

TRADITIONAL GRACE NOTE:

played as in classical music before the main note.

LAZY GRACE NOTE:

played on the beat together with the main note and released immediately while continuing to sustain the main note.

Try both types of grace notes in the following example.

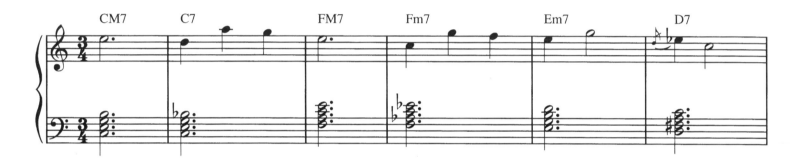

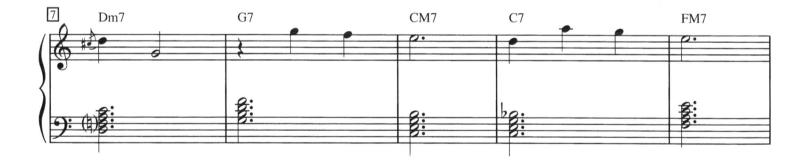

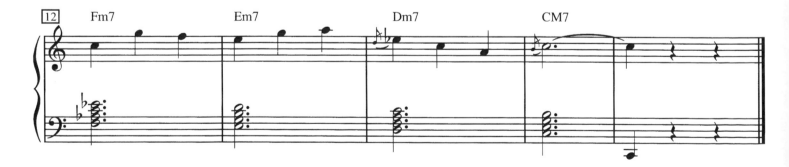

Play the above once again and add grace notes in other places.

Fake Books

Go to your local music store and ask to see a FAKE BOOK. This book will contain hundreds of popular song melodies; however, there will be no piano parts. The melody will appear with the chord symbols written above the measures. Sometimes the words are included. The jazz musician is required to "fake" or improvise an accompaniment.

Eventually you will want to purchase popular sheet music and fake books. By the time you complete this book you will know enough chords to play melodies with a block chord accompaniment. To help you, the appendix contains a listing of all chords.

How To Play From A Fake Book

The following is an example of how a melody looks in a fake book.

AMAZING GRACE

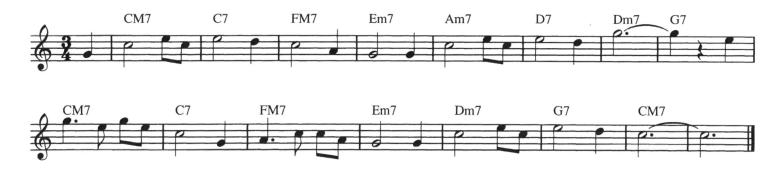

•Practice the melody.
•MEMORIZE the chords.
•Play both hands together with the block-chord style accompaniment.

The first two measures of "Amazing Grace":

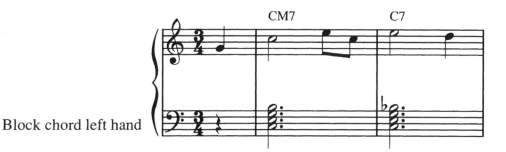

Block chord left hand

Improvise other accompaniments for "Amazing Grace".

Another Kind Of Blues

The MINOR BLUES scale provides additional material for blues improvisation. This scale produces a blues sound associated with the 80s and 90s.

C Minor Blues Scale

Play the 1 ♭3 4 ♯4(♭5) 5 ♭7 notes of any major scale.

Play the following exercise and listen to the sound of the minor blues scale.

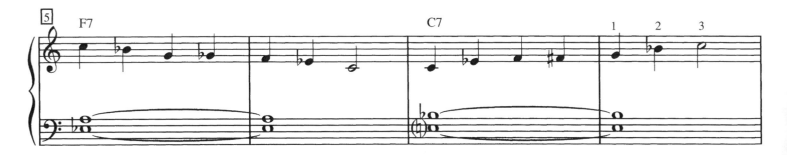

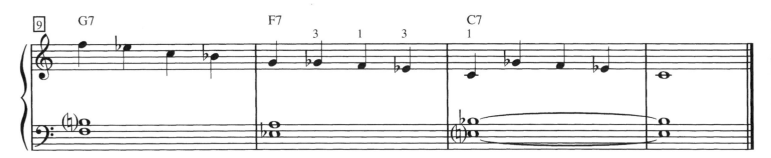

A rock improvisation based upon the notes of the C minor blues scale:

BLUSIE

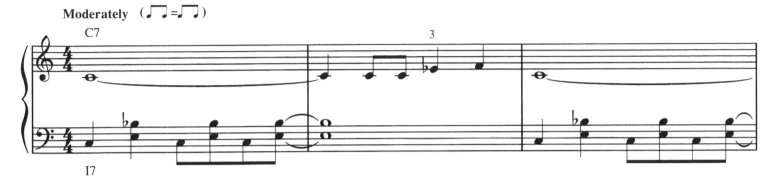

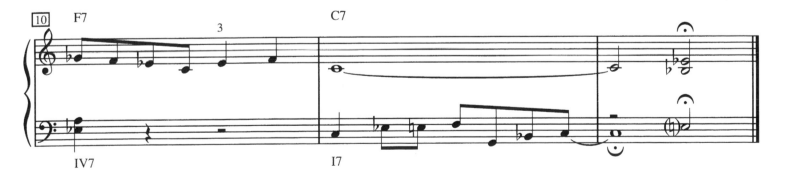

Blues Improvisation

Follow the improvising steps and create your own twelve-measure blues improvisation with the notes of the C minor blues scale.

- Start on any note
- End on the tonic
- Play notes in any order
- Repeat any note

Best left hand for now: third and flat seventh of the dominant seventh chords

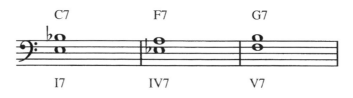

Follow the chart and improvise a twelve-measure blues with the C minor blues scale.

Play even eighth notes.

Improvise right hand.

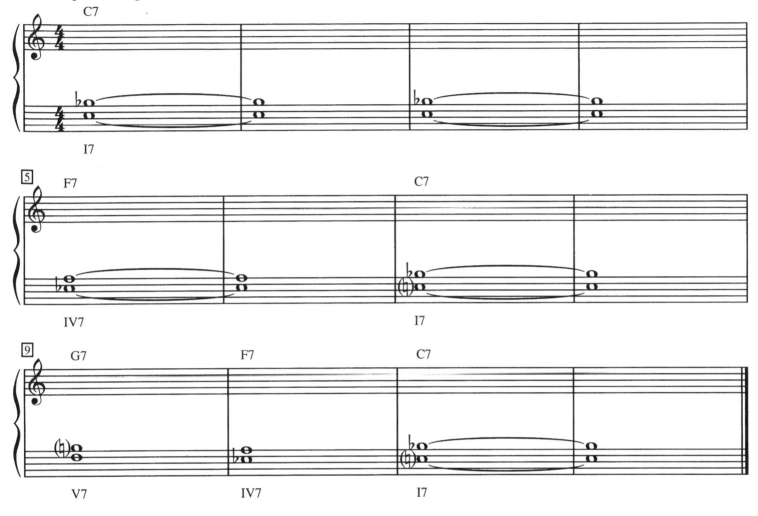

D Minor Blues Scale

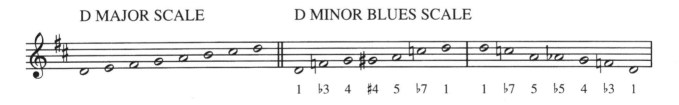

The following song applies the D minor blues scale to swing style in a minor key.

INTERPRETATION: Space quarter notes•Anticipated beats receive slight accents•Observe dynamics and maintain a steady beat•Play the left hand legato.

Practice Rhythm: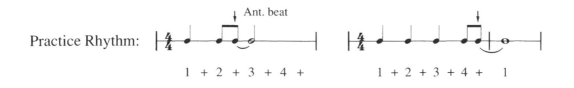

SWING THING

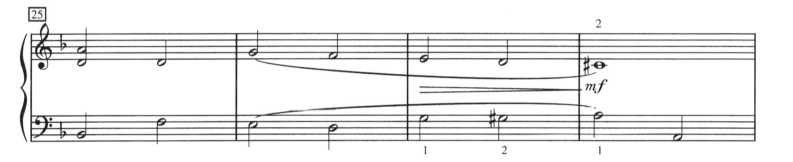

Play "Blusie" (pg. 75) and "Swing Thing" several times. Remember the sound of the minor blues scale. You will hear it often in swing and rock music.

Sixth Chords

FORMULA: Combine the 1 3 5 and 6 notes from the major scale.

Chord Symbol: 6

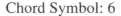

1 3 5 6

Augmented Chords

FORMULA: Combine the 1 3 #5 notes from the major scale.

Chord Symbol: + or aug.

1 3 #5

Fill in the chords in the blank measures.

Diminished Seventh Chords

Notice that the VII chord is a diminished triad. This chord is not used in jazz. Instead the seventh is added and the chord becomes a diminished seventh chord.

Chord Symbol: dim or ° (Ex: C°)

Only three different diminished seventh chords exist. It is easier to memorize the three chords than use a formula. Each inversion of the chord becomes another diminished seventh chord. The lowest note becomes the new root.

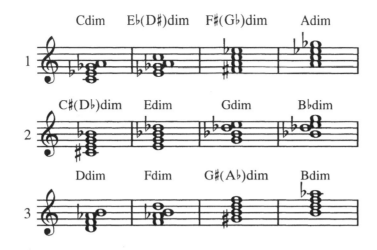

The following example applies the new chords. The sound is typical of the jazz music of the 40s and 50s.

The thought of memorizing so many chords can be overwhelming. Memorize chords as you need them for each song.

You now have a knowledge of enough chords to use a fake book successfully. Begin with slow three-four songs. Play block chord accompaniments. If the melody interferes with the left hand, play the melody an octave higher.

Some chord symbols will be presented in Book Two. In the meantime, refer to the chart below when unfamiliar chord symbols appear. The C chord will serve as an example, but any chord letter may be substituted.

WHEN YOU SEE:	PLAY:
C(add 9)	C6 or CM7
C9 or C13	C7
Cm6	Cm
Cm9 or Cm11	Cm7
C7+5	C+
C7♭5	C7
C7♭9	C7
C7♯9	C7

Boogie Woogie

Boogie, a jazz style of the 40s, is based on the blues chord progression. This style is sometimes called "eight to the bar" referring to the characteristic left-hand bass patterns with eight eighth notes to the measure.

Left-hand bass pattern:

Play the following exercise slowly to practice moving from one chord to the next. Gradually increase the tempo.

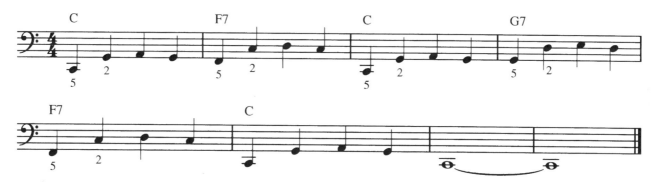

INTERPRETATION: Left hand legato • Space quarter notes • Eighth notes legato.

BOOGIE MAN

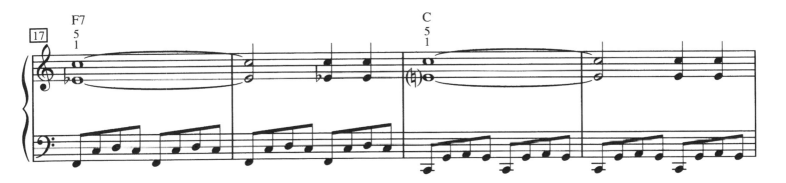

Jazz Pedal

Although there are many ways to decide when to change the pedal, the final judge on pedaling is the ear. If the music becomes blurred, use less pedal. LISTEN!

Exceptions always occur, but here are some general rules.

STYLE	PEDAL
Ragtime	none or very light
Swing	Fast: none Slow: light pedal
Rock	Fast: none Slow: yes
Boogie	none
Jazz Waltz	light pedal
Blues	Fast: none Slow: light pedal

Syncopated rhythms, which are usually spaced and accented, should not be pedaled. Pedal each time the chord changes.

The next song is a moderately slow rock ballad that requires pedal. The rhythm of the opening measures is the same as ragtime rhythm number three.

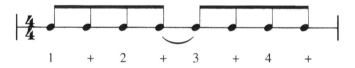

INTERPRETATION: Pedal the opening measures as indicated, using a blurred effect•Apply pedal rules to the next section•Don't blur notes; listen•The final four measures are pedaled like the introduction•Repeat this section as often as you wish and get softer•Watch out for dynamics.

OVER AND OUT

pedal on your own

Repeat and Fade

ped. simile

Appendix

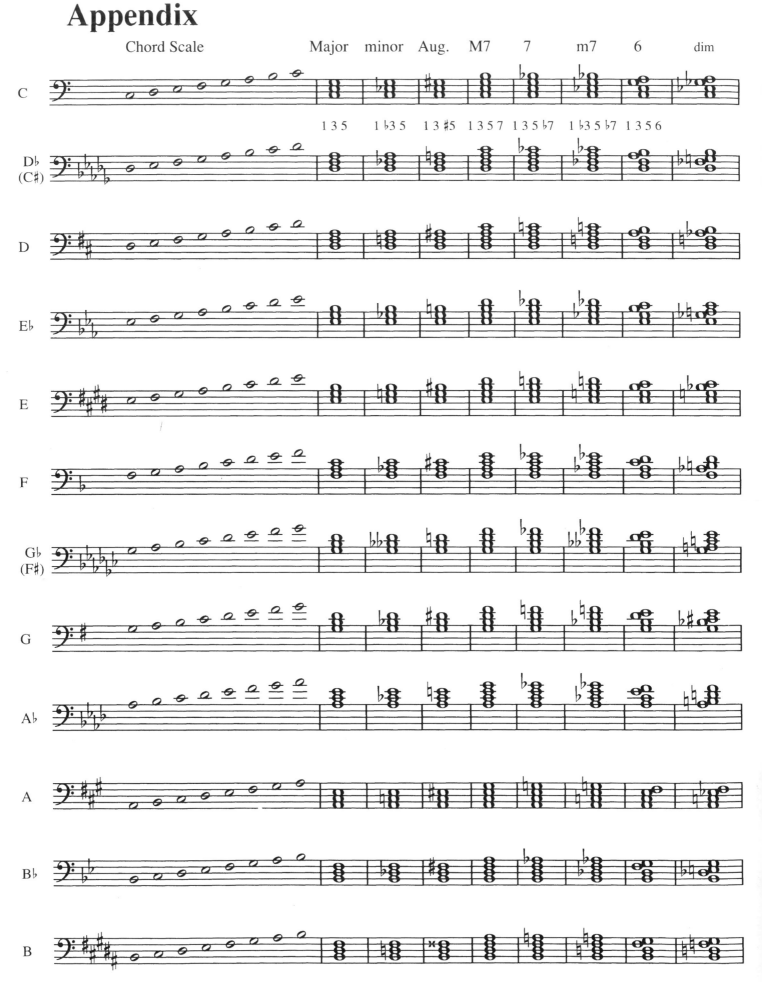

This series showcases great original piano music from our **Hal Leonard Student Piano Library** family of composers. Carefully graded for easy selection.

BILL BOYD

JAZZ BITS (AND PIECES)
Early Intermediate Level
00290312 11 Solos........................$7.99

JAZZ DELIGHTS
Intermediate Level
00240435 11 Solos........................$8.99

JAZZ FEST
Intermediate Level
00240436 10 Solos........................$8.99

JAZZ PRELIMS
Early Elementary Level
00290032 12 Solos........................$7.99

JAZZ SKETCHES
Intermediate Level
00220001 8 Solos........................$8.99

JAZZ STARTERS
Elementary Level
00290425 10 Solos........................$8.99

JAZZ STARTERS II
Late Elementary Level
00290434 11 Solos........................$7.99

JAZZ STARTERS III
Late Elementary Level
00290465 12 Solos........................$8.99

THINK JAZZ!
Early Intermediate Level
00290417 Method Book............$12.99

TONY CARAMIA

JAZZ MOODS
Intermediate Level
00296728 8 Solos........................$6.95

SUITE DREAMS
Intermediate Level
00296775 4 Solos........................$6.99

SONDRA CLARK

DAKOTA DAYS
Intermediate Level
00296521 5 Solos........................$6.95

FLORIDA FANTASY SUITE
Intermediate Level
00296766 3 Duets........................$7.95

THREE ODD METERS
Intermediate Level
00296472 3 Duets........................$6.95

MATTHEW EDWARDS

CONCERTO FOR YOUNG PIANISTS
FOR 2 PIANOS, FOUR HANDS
Intermediate Level Book/CD
00296356 3 Movements $19.99

CONCERTO NO. 2 IN G MAJOR
FOR 2 PIANOS, 4 HANDS
Intermediate Level Book/CD
00296670 3 Movements............$17.99

PHILLIP KEVEREN

MOUSE ON A MIRROR
Late Elementary Level
00296361 5 Solos........................$8.99

MUSICAL MOODS
Elementary/Late Elementary Level
00296714 7 Solos........................$6.99

SHIFTY-EYED BLUES
Late Elementary Level
00296374 5 Solos........................$7.99

CAROL KLOSE

THE BEST OF CAROL KLOSE
Early to Late Intermediate Level
00146151 15 Solos....................$12.99

CORAL REEF SUITE
Late Elementary Level
00296354 7 Solos........................$7.50

DESERT SUITE
Intermediate Level
00296667 6 Solos........................$7.99

FANCIFUL WALTZES
Early Intermediate Level
00296473 5 Solos........................$7.95

GARDEN TREASURES
Late Intermediate Level
00296787 5 Solos........................$8.50

ROMANTIC EXPRESSIONS
Intermediate to Late Intermediate Level
00296923 5 Solos........................$8.99

WATERCOLOR MINIATURES
Early Intermediate Level
00296848 7 Solos........................$7.99

JENNIFER LINN

AMERICAN IMPRESSIONS
Intermediate Level
00296471 6 Solos........................$8.99

ANIMALS HAVE FEELINGS TOO
Early Elementary/Elementary Level
00147789 8 Solos........................$8.99

AU CHOCOLAT
Late Elementary/Early Intermediate Level
00298110 7 Solos........................$8.99

CHRISTMAS IMPRESSIONS
Intermediate Level
00296706 8 Solos........................$8.99

JUST PINK
Elementary Level
00296722 9 Solos........................$8.99

LES PETITES IMAGES
Late Elementary Level
00296664 7 Solos........................$8.99

LES PETITES IMPRESSIONS
Intermediate Level
00296355 6 Solos........................$8.99

REFLECTIONS
Late Intermediate Level
00296843 5 Solos........................$8.99

TALES OF MYSTERY
Intermediate Level
00296769 6 Solos........................$8.99

LYNDA LYBECK-ROBINSON

ALASKA SKETCHES
Early Intermediate Level
00119637 8 Solos........................$8.99

AN AWESOME ADVENTURE
Late Elementary Level
00137563 8 Solos........................$7.99

FOR THE BIRDS
Early Intermediate/Intermediate Level
00237078 9 Solos........................$8.99

WHISPERING WOODS
Late Elementary Level
00275905 9 Solos........................$8.99

MONA REJINO

CIRCUS SUITE
Late Elementary Level
00296665 5 Solos........................$8.99

COLOR WHEEL
Early Intermediate Level
00201951 6 Solos........................$9.99

IMPRESIONES DE ESPAÑA
Intermediate Level
00337520 6 Solos........................$8.99

IMPRESSIONS OF NEW YORK
Intermediate Level
00364212........................$8.99

JUST FOR KIDS
Elementary Level
00296840 8 Solos........................$7.99

MERRY CHRISTMAS MEDLEYS
Intermediate Level
00296799 5 Solos........................$8.99

MINIATURES IN STYLE
Intermediate Level
00148088 6 Solos........................$8.99

PORTRAITS IN STYLE
Early Intermediate Level
00296507 6 Solos........................$8.99

EUGÉNIE ROCHEROLLE

CELEBRATION SUITE
Intermediate Level
00152724 3 Duets........................$8.99

ENCANTOS ESPAÑOLES (SPANISH DELIGHTS)
Intermediate Level
00125451 6 Solos........................$8.99

JAMBALAYA
Intermediate Level
00296654 2 Pianos, 8 Hands.....$12.99
00296725 2 Pianos, 4 Hands.......$7.95

JEROME KERN CLASSICS
Intermediate Level
00296577 10 Solos....................$12.99

LITTLE BLUES CONCERTO
Early Intermediate Level
00142801 2 Pianos, 4 Hands......$12.99

TOUR FOR TWO
Late Elementary Level
00296832 6 Duets........................$9.99

TREASURES
Late Elementary/Early Intermediate Level
00296924 7 Solos........................$8.99

JEREMY SISKIND

BIG APPLE JAZZ
Intermediate Level
00278209 8 Solos........................$8.99

MYTHS AND MONSTERS
Late Elementary/Early Intermediate Level
00148148 9 Solos........................$8.99

CHRISTOS TSITSAROS

DANCES FROM AROUND THE WORLD
Early Intermediate Level
00296688 7 Solos........................$8.99

FIVE SUMMER PIECES
Late Intermediate/Advanced Level
00361235 5 Solos....................$12.99

LYRIC BALLADS
Intermediate/Late Intermediate Level
00102404 6 Solos........................$8.99

POETIC MOMENTS
Intermediate Level
00296403 8 Solos........................$8.99

SEA DIARY
Early Intermediate Level
00253486 9 Solos........................$8.99

SONATINA HUMORESQUE
Late Intermediate Level
00296772 3 Movements............$6.99

SONGS WITHOUT WORDS
Intermediate Level
00296506 9 Solos........................$9.99

THREE PRELUDES
Early Advanced Level
00130747 3 Solos........................$8.99

THROUGHOUT THE YEAR
Late Elementary Level
00296723 12 Duets....................$6.95

ADDITIONAL COLLECTIONS

AT THE LAKE
by Elvina Pearce
Elementary/Late Elementary Level
00131642 10 Solos and Duets.....$7.99

CHRISTMAS FOR TWO
by Dan Fox
Early Intermediate Level
00290069 13 Duets....................$8.99

CHRISTMAS JAZZ
by Mike Springer
Intermediate Level
00296525 6 Solos........................$8.99

COUNTY RAGTIME FESTIVAL
by Fred Kern
Intermediate Level
00296882 7 Solos........................$7.99

LITTLE JAZZERS
by Jennifer Watts
Elementary/Late Elementary Level
00154573 9 Solos........................$8.99

PLAY THE BLUES!
by Luann Carman
Early Intermediate Level
00296357 10 Solos....................$9.99

ROLLER COASTERS & RIDES
by Jennifer & Mike Watts
Intermediate Level
00131144 8 Duets........................$8.99

www.halleonard.com

Prices, contents, and availability subject
to change without notice.

POPULAR SONGS
HAL LEONARD STUDENT PIANO LIBRARY

The **Hal Leonard Student Piano Library** has great songs, and you will find all your favorites here: Disney classics, Broadway and movie favorites, and today's top hits. These graded collections are skillfully and imaginatively arranged for students and pianists at every level, from elementary solos with teacher accompaniments to sophisticated piano solos for the advancing pianist.

Adele
arr. Mona Rejino
Correlates with HLSPL Level 5
00159590..............................$12.99

The Beatles
arr. Eugénie Rocherolle
Correlates with HLSPL Level 5
00296649..............................$12.99

Irving Berlin Piano Duos
arr. Don Heitler and Jim Lyke
Correlates with HLSPL Level 5
00296838..............................$14.99

Broadway Favorites
arr. Phillip Keveren
Correlates with HLSPL Level 4
00279192..............................$12.99

Chart Hits
arr. Mona Rejino
Correlates with HLSPL Level 5
00296710..............................$8.99

Christmas at the Piano
arr. Lynda Lybeck-Robinson
Correlates with HLSPL Level 4
00298194..............................$12.99

Christmas Cheer
arr. Phillip Keveren
Correlates with HLSPL Level 4
00296616..............................$8.99

Classic Christmas Favorites
arr. Jennifer & Mike Watts
Correlates with HLSPL Level 5
00129582..............................$9.99

Christmas Time Is Here
arr. Eugénie Rocherolle
Correlates with HLSPL Level 5
00296614..............................$8.99

Classic Joplin Rags
arr. Fred Kern
Correlates with HLSPL Level 5
00296743..............................$9.99

Classical Pop – Lady Gaga Fugue & Other Pop Hits
arr. Giovanni Dettori
Correlates with HLSPL Level 5
00296921..............................$12.99

Contemporary Movie Hits
arr. by Carol Klose, Jennifer Linn and Wendy Stevens
Correlates with HLSPL Level 5
00296780..............................$8.99

Contemporary Pop Hits
arr. Wendy Stevens
Correlates with HLSPL Level 3
00296836..............................$8.99

Cool Pop
arr. Mona Rejino
Correlates with HLSPL Level 5
00360103..............................$12.99

Country Favorites
arr. Mona Rejino
Correlates with HLSPL Level 5
00296861..............................$9.99

Disney Favorites
arr. Phillip Keveren
Correlates with HLSPL Levels 3/4
00296647..............................$10.99

Disney Film Favorites
arr. Mona Rejino
Correlates with HLSPL Level 5
00296809 ....$10.99

Disney Piano Duets
arr. Jennifer & Mike Watts
Correlates with HLSPL Level 5
00113759..............................$13.99

Double Agent! Piano Duets
arr. Jeremy Siskind
Correlates with HLSPL Level 5
00121595..............................$12.99

Easy Christmas Duets
arr. Mona Rejino & Phillip Keveren
Correlates with HLSPL Levels 3/4
00237139..............................$9.99

Easy Disney Duets
arr. Jennifer and Mike Watts
Correlates with HLSPL Level 4
00243727..............................$12.99

Four Hands on Broadway
arr. Fred Kern
Correlates with HLSPL Level 5
00146177..............................$12.99

Frozen Piano Duets
arr. Mona Rejino
Correlates with HLSPL Levels 3/4
00144294..............................$12.99

Hip-Hop for Piano Solo
arr. Logan Evan Thomas
Correlates with HLSPL Level 5
00360950..............................$12.99

Jazz Hits for Piano Duet
arr. Jeremy Siskind
Correlates with HLSPL Level 5
00143248..............................$12.99

Elton John
arr. Carol Klose
Correlates with HLSPL Level 5
00296721..............................$10.99

Joplin Ragtime Duets
arr. Fred Kern
Correlates with HLSPL Level 5
00296771..............................$8.99

Movie Blockbusters
arr. Mona Rejino
Correlates with HLSPL Level 5
00232850..............................$10.99

The Nutcracker Suite
arr. Lynda Lybeck-Robinson
Correlates with HLSPL Levels 3/4
00147906..............................$8.99

Pop Hits for Piano Duet
arr. Jeremy Siskind
Correlates with HLSPL Level 5
00224734..............................$12.99

Sing to the King
arr. Phillip Keveren
Correlates with HLSPL Level 5
00296808..............................$8.99

Smash Hits
arr. Mona Rejino
Correlates with HLSPL Level 5
00284841..............................$10.99

Spooky Halloween Tunes
arr. Fred Kern
Correlates with HLSPL Levels 3/4
00121550..............................$9.99

Today's Hits
arr. Mona Rejino
Correlates with HLSPL Level 5
00296646..............................$9.99

Top Hits
arr. Jennifer and Mike Watts
Correlates with HLSPL Level 5
00296894..............................$10.99

Top Piano Ballads
arr. Jennifer Watts
Correlates with HLSPL Level 5
00197926..............................$10.99

Video Game Hits
arr. Mona Rejino
Correlates with HLSPL Level 4
00300310..............................$12.99

You Raise Me Up
arr. Deborah Brady
Correlates with HLSPL Level 2/3
00296576..............................$7.95

HAL•LEONARD®
7777 W. BLUEMOUND RD. P.O. BOX 13819 MILWAUKEE, WI 53213

Prices, contents and availability subject to change without notice. Prices may vary outside the U.S.

Visit our website at www.halleonard.com